Contents

Stiff materials 4

Bendy materials 8

Stiff and bendy materials 12

Quiz 22

Picture glossary 23

Index 24

Stiff materials

Some things are stiff.

Stiff things can be hard.

Stiff things cannot bend.

Stiff things cannot stretch.

Bendy materials

Some things are bendy.

Bendy things can be hard or soft.

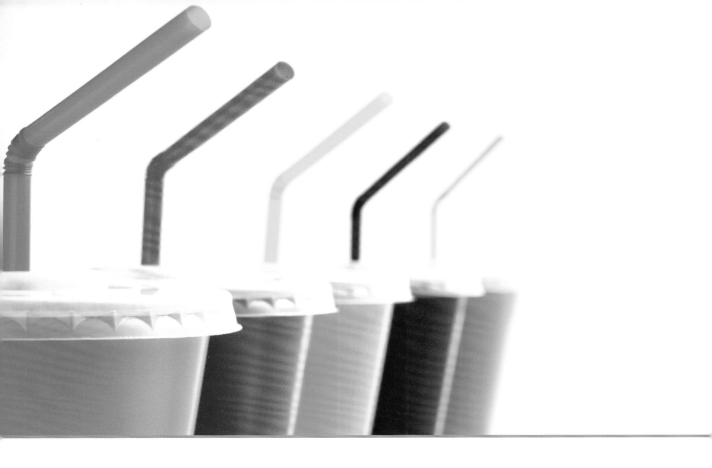

Bendy things can bend.

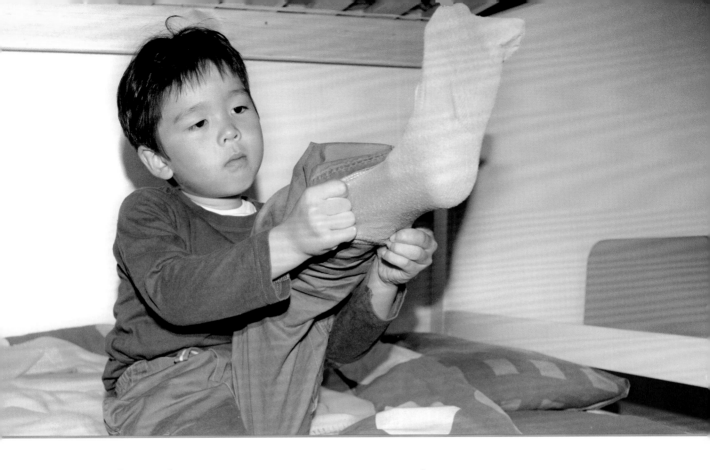

Bendy things can stretch.

Stiff and bendy materials

Plastic can be stiff.

You cannot bend stiff plastic.

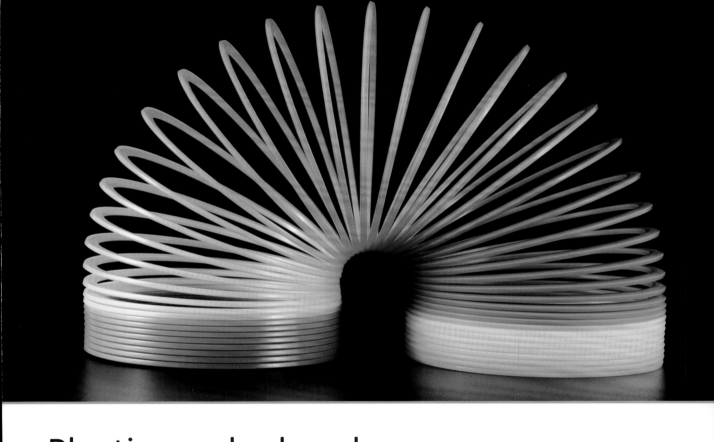

Plastic can be bendy.

You can bend bendy plastic.

Glass is stiff.

You cannot stretch it.

Rubber is bendy.
You can stretch it.

Wood is stiff.

You cannot stretch it.

Wool is bendy.
You can stretch it.

You can tell if something is stiff or bendy.

You can feel if something is stiff
or bendy.

You can see if something is stiff or bendy.

We can see when things are stiff.
We can see when things are bendy.

Quiz

Which of these things are stiff?
Which of these things are bendy?

Picture glossary

 **bendy** material that can bend without breaking

 **plastic** material that can be soft or hard

 **stiff** hard to bend or move

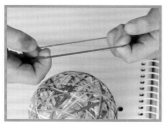 **stretch** make something longer or wider, especially by pulling

Index

glass 14   wood 16

plastic 12, 13   wool 17

rubber 15

Note to parents and teachers
Before reading
Tell children that materials can be stiff or bendy. Ask children if they know what "stiff" and "bendy" mean. Pass around several objects and ask children to guess if they are stiff or bendy. Possible objects could be modelling clay, paper, pencil, spoon, scarf, bricks, straw, a glass, and a plastic cup.

After reading
Help children to make an object out of modelling clay. Mix 500 grams of flour and 273 grams of salt in a bowl. Add water (about 237 millilitres) gradually to form a ball. Knead until it no longer falls apart. As children are moulding their clay, ask them if their clay is bendy or stiff. Let their objects dry at room temperature for a couple of days. After they harden, ask the children if they are bendy or stiff. When the clay has completely hardened, let the children paint their objects.